W9-AUN-314

St. Patrick's Day

Josie Keogh

PowerKiDS
press

New York

For the Beirne family

Published in 2013 by The Rosen Publishing Group, Inc.
29 East 21st Street, New York, NY 10010

First Edition

Editor: Amelie von Zumbusch
Book Design: Andrew Povolny

Photo Credits: Cover R. Nelson/Flickr/Getty Images; pp. 5, 17 © iStockphoto.com/Liza McCorkle; p. 7 Martin Gray/National Geographic/Getty Images; p. 9 Time Life Pictures/Getty Images; p. 11 Terrie L. Zeller/Shutterstock.com; p. 13 KidStock/Blend Images/Getty Images; p. 15 Ken Ilio/Flickr/Getty Images; p. 19 Goodshoot/Thinkstock; p. 21 Stuart Monk/Shutterstock.com; p. 23 Vsevolod33/Shutterstock.com.

Library of Congress Cataloging-in-Publication Data

Keogh, Josie.
 St. Patrick's Day / by Josie Keogh. — 1st ed.
   p. cm. — (Powerkids readers: happy holidays!)
 Includes index.
 ISBN 978-1-4488-9628-8 (library binding) — ISBN 978-1-4488-9714-8 (pbk.) —
 ISBN 978-1-4488-9715-5 (6-pack)
 1. Saint Patrick's Day—Juvenile literature. I. Title.
 GT4995.S3K46 2013
 394.262—dc23
                                       2012022309

Manufactured in the United States of America

CPSIA Compliance Information: Batch #W13PK3: For Further Information contact Rosen Publishing, New York, New York at 1-800-237-9932

Contents

It is St. Patrick's Day!

4

Patrick was an Irish saint.

He was born in Britain.

PATRICK

9

Draw a **shamrock**.

Eat a treat!

The Chicago River gets
dyed green!

Green stands for Ireland.

Eire is the Irish name
for Ireland.

New York has the
biggest **parade**.

A **step dance** competition is a feis.

WORDS TO KNOW

parade

shamrock

step dance

INDEX

WEBSITES

Due to the changing nature of Internet links, PowerKids Press has developed an online list of websites related to the subject of this book. This site is updated regularly. Please use this link to access the list:
www.powerkidslinks.com/pkrhh/stpa/